Balanced Life
Living Life From Within

Darvis R. Simms and Alisha Lalji

Printed in the United States of America

First Printing, 2015

ISBN 978-1-312-84063-8

Publisher, Darvis Simms
13214 Ashford Park Drive
Raleigh, NC 27613

darvis@foreverfitfirm.com

Distributor, Lulu Press, Inc.

This book is dedicated to all the spiritual teachers from whom I have learned the Truth which has set me free.

ACKNOWLEDGMENTS

I would like to acknowledge Alisha Lalji without whom this book could not have been written. Alisha, thank you for wise words, your patience, and your support.

CONTENTS

INTRODUCTION

Ever feel as if there is no purpose to your life and each day is just the same as yesterday? Do you feel you struggle through life while others have it so easy? Ever ask yourself why am I trying so hard and nothing seems to go right for me? What about that empty feeling you have and nothing you do seems to satisfy it? Ever watch the news and think that if God is real why is the world so messed up?

If you've ever felt any of these things you are not alone. Everyone struggles at times to find meaning in their life. If you've ever felt like you are on a journey and you have no idea of where it will end, then this book is for you.

Some people seem to breeze through life as if they have a guide that's always showing them the easy way. There is such a life force. This way of living will bring you peace and harmony in all aspects of your life and if that is what you seek, then read on.

As early as I can remember I always felt a presence with me something within me that was an internal guide. Whenever I would follow that internal guidance things would turn out well for me no matter the circumstance I found myself in. For instance, when I was around age seven, being rambunctious as kids are at that age, I was playing with a pair of scissors and accidently punctured a hole in my mother's brand new sofa. I was so afraid to tell my mother what had happened that I made up all kinds of stories in my head of what to say to her. Then this inner guide gently said, "Tell your mother the truth and all will be okay." So I did. My mother was understandably upset at seeing the hole in her new sofa, but she assured me that everyone makes mistakes and that she loved me far more than a sofa. She was proud of me for telling the truth. Ever since that day I have sought that internal guidance in all that I do.

I now know the internal guide in me is Divine Love and Divine Love loves me in spite of the mistakes I make. It understands just as my mother did when I put a hole in her brand new sofa. This same Divine Love resides in everyone and is simply awaiting our recognition of It.

The Divine Love I'm talking about permeates all life. It is the Invisible Life Force that animates and governs all we see—from the movement of the heavenly bodies, to the changing of the seasons, to the beating of one's heart. Some call this Life Force God, some call it Spirit, and others call it Universal Life. No matter what you call it, you must realize it is Everywhere

Present, All Knowing, and All Powerful in order to fully benefit from It in your life. This Life Force created, maintains, and sustains you. It is the intelligence that orchestrates the billions of interactions that happen in your body each day that keeps you alive.

You have unlimited access to this awesome Life Force through your consciousness. As a matter of fact, this Life Force beckons you to recognize it. It stands always ready to come to your aid, but it will not come unless invited. It knows how to guide you easily and harmoniously in accomplishing all your tasks, both great and small.

You exist as an expression of this great Life Force as spirit, mind, and body. In order to live a fulfilled and joyful life you need to recognize and balance these three dimensions. There is a rhythm to life that once entered and maintained, makes things flow easily and harmoniously with little stress.

The object of this book is to help you understand this Life Force, and how to be in tune with It to create the life you truly desire. Take a journey with me and transform your body, mind, and spirit. We will explore balance from the inside out starting with spiritual energy, the spiritual laws and mental energy. Then my co-author, Alisha Lalji, will share the healing modalities that completely transformed her life. The latter part of the book will start a conversation about health, fitness and nutrition—all subjects especially dear to me since I'm a personal trainer. Alisha and I thank you for taking this journey of health and well-being with us and can't wait to hear about your results.

"All things were made by Him; and without Him was not any thing made that was made. In Him was life; and the life was the light of men." —John 1:3-4.

DISCLAIMER

All information and tools presented within this book are intended for educational purposes. Any health, diet or exercise advice is not intended as medical diagnosis or treatment. If you think you have any type of medical condition you must seek professional advice.

1 SPIRITUAL ENERGY

You are an energetic being made up of spirit, mind, and body. You exist as spiritual, mental, and physical energy. All three of these energies vibrate at different frequencies and must be balanced in order for you to live a happy, balanced, and fulfilled life.

The single most important concept to comprehend is that human consciousness is now a theoretically quantifiable phenomenon and at least partially measurable as an electromagnetic energy field radiating out from the human body.. (**William L. Smith**. *Journal of Theoretics, Vol. 4-2)*

You are one with the Divine and one with the energy of this invisible spirit first and foremost. Thus, you are united with all of life. This is the access point to a rhythm of life that is humanly incomprehensible. As you become aware of the energy of your spiritual existence, the stress and strain of daily life begin to fade.

You are a part of the Eternal Divine Spirit which is the life behind all things. This is where the energy resides that orchestrates all life. It keeps the planets in alignment, causes the sun to rise, provides the air that you breathe and is the core of your very existence. This Loving Presence is always working on your behalf for It created you out of Itself. It contains the answer to your every problem, and it provides for your every need. It resides in you and all you need do is connect with this Loving Presence and It will guide you easily and harmoniously through life.

*A human being is a part of the whole, called by us the Universe, a part limited in time and space. He experiences himself, his thoughts and feelings as something separated from the rest- a kind of optical delusion of his consciousness. This delusion is a kind of prison for us, restricting us to our personal desires and to affection for a few persons nearest to us. Our task must be to free ourselves from this prison by widening our circles of compassion to embrace all living creatures and the whole of nature in its beauty. Nobody is able to achieve this completely, but the striving for such achievement is in itself a part of the liberation and of a foundation for inner security. (**Albert Einstein**, N.Y. Post, November 28, 1972)*

In your access to Universal Life through your spiritual energy you have access to unlimited possibility. This is where the highest energy of all life resides. This is Love. In the energy of Love you will find all the things that make for a happy, balanced, and fulfilled life. For you were created to express this Loving Energy in all that you do and this Loving Energy is forever seeking to express Itself as good in and through your life. This Love is the heart of your existence and is only limited by your consciousness of It.

This Loving Presence is always ready to reveal Itself in the form of whatever you need, but it cannot do for you anymore than you allow it to do. For what it does for you it must express in and through you. Thus, the greater your awareness of this Presence, the greater the good in all forms you receive in and through your life.

If you use this consciousness of Love as your starting place each day you will find that your daily tasks will flow easily and harmoniously with very little stress and strain. For this Loving Presence has unlimited organizing power to bring about results in your life with very little effort on your part.

I start my day in this consciousness of Love. I wake up 45 minutes early, make my coffee, and read something inspirational. Then I sit quietly and contemplate the meaning of the passage I just read. In that time of silence the answers to my life's problems unfold before my feet. I call this my morning coffee with God.

One day in my morning coffee with God I was made aware that the air I was breathing was the source of my physical existence and without it I would quickly die. Yet, I never took any thought about whether or not I always had air to breathe, but I worried about things like my health, having enough money, my relationships, etc. Then I was assured that if I trusted in the Divine to provide for my every need in life just as I trusted It to supply the air I breathe, I would never have to worry about a thing. Thus, I realized that trusting in God for my every need was the key to connecting and manifesting the life I truly desired.

2 SPIRITUAL LAWS

In order for you to benefit from your spiritual energy you must realize there are spiritual laws just as there are physical laws. These spiritual laws are always at work in your life creating the conditions and circumstances which surround you. Learning what these spiritual laws are and abiding by them will greatly change your life.

As I mentioned before, everything that is in physical form is first created by the invisible energy of spirit. There are principles through which spiritual energy works to create the physical things that you can see, touch, hear, smell, and taste, as well as the emotional things you feel. You use these principles everyday, whether you know it or not. The problem is most people don't know that these spiritual principles exist. They use them in ignorance, thus creating conditions in their lives that are sometimes favorable, sometimes not. However, when you learn to use the spiritual laws correctly you begin to create the life of your dreams.

The discovery of spiritual laws was huge for me. I spent many years trying unsuccessfully to change unwanted conditions in my life. I wondered what I was doing wrong. Then one day I was browsing through the self-help section of my local bookstore and found *Thoughts are Things* by Ernest Holmes. I bought the book and devoured it in a few days. In that book Holmes simply explains that your inner world of thoughts creates your outer world of life conditions. That resonated with me and I analyzed my inner thoughts and beliefs. I realized I needed to change the way I was thinking in order to be successful at changing unwanted conditions in my life. By changing the way I thought I noticed the conditions of my life conforming to my new way of thinking. At this point I began my search/journey to learn about spiritual laws and how they work.

Cause and Effect

Wholistic, or holistic, awareness remains beyond linear time and three dimensional space, and therefore is not easily recognized. We must practice this wholistic experience in order to recognize it. Our language, and our old ideas or paradigms, still limit our growth. Meditation and many other practices, like YXQ, are ways of transcending the limitations of the linear mind in order to experience the multidimensionality of interconnectedness, and to experience our oneness with the universal energy, the unified field, or consciousness. (**Gloria Alvino**, *ordained minister and a counselor on healing into dying/healing into living*)

The Law of Cause and Effect, (also known as the Law of Attraction) basically says that there is an invisible cause (thoughts and beliefs) behind every effect (condition or circumstance) in your life. In order to change the condition or circumstance you must first change the thought and belief. You live within two planes, an inner world of your thoughts and beliefs and an outer world of conditions and circumstances in your life. The conditions and circumstances of your outer world are always a reflection of your inner world of thoughts and beliefs. The Law of Cause and Effect is always in balance in your life, thus, you cannot experience an effect in your life without an underlying cause. Thus the saying, "Your thoughts create your reality."

The conditions and circumstances of your life, be they disease, poverty, or conflict in your relationships, can never be changed in the outer world of their appearance; they can only be changed in the inner world of your thoughts and beliefs. Your inner world of thoughts and beliefs is where you create the conditions of your life and it is the only place where you can change them. As the mystics say, "If you want to change the world, you must change yourself first."

Most people live their lives responding to events and conditions that they created themselves via their thinking and belief system. For example, you get into a fight with your best friend about some situation that ends your friendship. You think you don't need that person in your life and you move on. Eventually you find another best friend and after some time you have a fight with them about the same issue and also end that friendship. You go through a series of friendships just to have them end over the same situation and you think that no one understands you. You think the problem is with your friends while all the time you have created the condition somewhere in your mind that ends your friendships.

The example above could be any other situation that you repeatedly find yourself in. The solution cannot be found in trying to change the situation at the level of its appearance; you'll just get more of the same condition recycled in different venues. Somewhere in your inner thought and belief system you are giving life to the situation. But I hear you say, "I would never intentionally bring any bad situation into my life." However, you do through your misuse of the Law of Cause and Effect. Every condition and circumstance in your life is but a reflection of what's going on in your inner thoughts and beliefs. Therefore, the problem can never be solved from without; it can only be solved from within. The question is what thoughts are you harboring which are causing a reality you do not desire?

Using the Law of Cause and Effect to Create the Life You Want

The first thing you must do to properly use the Law of Cause and Effect is to create the things in your life you desire. This is a very sobering reality. You have to realize that you are responsible for every condition in your life be it labeled good or bad. The conditions and circumstances that presently surround you are a sum total of your inner thoughts and beliefs. Thus, you are never a victim of anything that appears in your life because you have called whatever it is into your life via your inner thoughts and beliefs.

I know the above statements are hard to digest, but they must be in order to use the Law of Cause and Effect intelligently. God has given you the power to create the world that you live in by giving you the capacity to think. You are always thinking and thus always creating and giving life and energy to your thoughts. The problem is that most people are not conscious of this truth and think random thoughts and so create random conditions in their lives. They believe they are the victims of random circumstances and conditions. The irony is THEY created the conditions themselves and when they try to change the conditions at the level of their appearance they create more of the unwanted condition.

For instance, if you desire to be in a relationship, but think it's really hard to find the right person, life will present you with that circumstance. In other words, life will give you what you do not want just as readily as it will give you what you want. That's why it's important to focus on what you do want in life and always be positive.

Think of it like this: you are the writer, producer, and director of a play called Your Life. You write the script, you set the scenes, and cast all the characters in this play through your thoughts and beliefs. Every person in the play of your life is only reading from the script you wrote for them.

Every situation that happens in your life is from the script you have already written in your mind. The good news is if you don't like the play you can re-write the script at any time.

Nothing happens randomly in your life. Everything that you experience you have written as a part of your script in your thoughts and beliefs. Therefore, it is pointless to try to fight against circumstances that you created. Just as it is pointless trying to make your reflection in a mirror smile while you are frowning. The experiences of your life are only a reflection of your inner thoughts and beliefs.

Meditation and Self-contemplation

In order to use the Law of Cause and Effect to create harmony in your life you have to learn to quiet your mind and control your thoughts. Your mind is constantly bombarded with thoughts. While you cannot stop thinking, you can control your thoughts, for you are the thinker and the number one gatekeeper of the thoughts you're allowing to enter your mind.

You learn to control your thoughts through the regular practice of sitting in silence. Some people call this meditation, I call it self-contemplation. This is the most proven way to access your spiritual energy which is your true identity. Your spiritual energy will always reveal truth in your life, showing you errors in your thoughts and beliefs which materialize as inharmonious conditions in your life. Meditation is a top down approach to making changes in your life with the least effort.

Sitting in silence can be very difficult at first, because your mind is filled with chatter and you are constantly jumping from one thought to another. Thoughts are like little children competing for your attention, they say "look at me, look at me" and you have to train yourself to only pay attention to the thoughts you want to grow in your mental garden. Don't get discouraged. The mental practice of silence is just like physical exercise, you get stronger and better at it the more you do it. Here are some techniques for learning to control your thoughts.

- Go to a quiet place where you will not be interrupted for about 30 minutes. Sit upright in a comfortable chair. Close your eyes, take deep controlled breaths, and slowly count backwards from 100 to zero. The counting will cause your mind to focus on the numbers and shut out any other distracting thoughts.

- While in your quiet place for 30 minutes, while you are closing your eyes and taking deep controlled breaths, think about your favorite outdoor spot. It could be the beach, the mountains, or watching a beautiful sunset. Imagine that you are physically at your favorite place. Hear the birds singing, feel the sun on your skin, experience the sound of the waves crashing on the shore. The object is to train your mind to focus on one thought at a time.

- Take a relaxing walk in nature. Listen to the birds sing, marvel at the beauty of the trees, flowers, and plant life. Again, the object is to train your mind to focus on one thought at a time.

- As I mentioned earlier, my favorite technique for quieting my mind is to read some inspirational passage and then to contemplate its meaning.

You will find that once you become efficient at quieting your mind, things will be revealed to you. It could be the solution to some situation that you've been struggling with, or the vision of completing a project. Whatever is revealed to you in these times of silence comes from the core of your existence and from your unity with the Divine. Trust that it is right for you.

The Law of Detachment

The Law of Detachment says not to be attached to the material things in your life, be it person, place or thing. For you give your power to whatever it is you are attached to. When you are attached to material things you spend your efforts trying to hold onto those things. You place your trust and security in a thing and not in your Inner-Self which is the only place lasting security can be found.

Real security is in your connection with your Inner-Self which knows how to manifest and provide for your every need. As previously stated in the Law of Cause and Effect, the things that surround your life are manifestations of your thoughts and beliefs. Thus, as you change your thought patterns and beliefs the things in your life change accordingly. Therefore, things are temporal, corresponding to your level of consciousness of the Divine's limitless substance and supply.

For example, at one time in my life I was plagued with too much credit card debt. Because I was self-employed and owned my own business, I depended on using my credit cards in lean times. As my balances began to grow I knew I had to put an end to my dependence on credit. So, one morning in my quiet time I was led to cut up all my credit cards and toss them in the trash. What transpired was amazing. New business started to flow in and my bank account balance started to increase proportionately. I now realize that I had placed my security in my attachment to using the credit cards instead my Inner-Self which knew how to increase my income. Thus, I was holding my consciousness, and in turn my income, at the level in which I thought I had to use credit.

The Divine is always ready, willing and able to meet your every need in life, but It can only give you what you are ready to receive. Thus, when you become attached to something, you keep your consciousness at the level of the thing you are attached to and you stifle your growth. You see, when you place your security in a person, place, or thing you limit your access to Divine substance and supply because you hold your consciousness in a static place.

For example, some people are attached to money and they spend most of their time and effort trying to keep it and to accumulate more of it. But no matter how much money they accumulate they are not secure because they are always afraid of losing it. They place their faith in the amount of money they have in their financial investments and spend their time worrying about every fluctuation in the financial markets. They become a prisoner of their attachment to money and their fear of losing the money eventually manifest into it being lost. As I said before, your thoughts create your reality.

Another example is people who are attached to a luxurious lifestyle. They live in the huge beautiful homes, drive the luxury cars, and send their children to the best private schools. They have accumulated everything that should make for a happy life, but most of them are not. They are unhappy in their marriages, unhappy in their careers, or unhappy with the business they have created and they are unwilling to change anything for fear of losing the lifestyle they have attained. They are prisoners of a false sense of security and have traded their happiness for the symbols of material success.

I'm not advocating that you should not enjoy having money and the luxuries of life. I'm saying that you can have the money, the lifestyle, and happiness too if you practice the Law of Detachment. Happiness is found in the right relationship to things in your life. The Divine wants you to have a happy, healthy, and fulfilled life. However, you can never find these qualities in material things, for these qualities come from an inner knowing that you have access to a Divine Power that fulfills and meets your every need.

Most people assume that to be spiritual minded means you must let go of the material things in life. In actuality, the Divine wants you to have abundance in all areas of your life and this includes material things as well. What you must be concerned with is how you look at material things and your attachment to them.

I believe each of us is born with a special gift inside of us. There is something that you can do better than anyone else in the world and when you reach inside yourself and give that special gift to the world you are happy and fulfilled. The security you are looking for is contained in the giving of your gift and you cannot release your talents while being attached to temporal things because you will spend all your energy trying to keep things as they are.

As crazy as this may sound, the only security you will find in life is in uncertainty and non-attachment. When you are certain that a thing is your salvation, you lock your consciousness at that level and you live your life within the limited boundaries you have created for yourself. On the other hand, there is unlimited possibility in uncertainty and non-attachment, for the Divine in you is saying all that I have is yours and you can have all that you are conscious of receiving.

How to Practice the Law of Detachment

You put the Law of Detachment to work in your life by realizing that you are the creator of all your life experiences via your belief system (consciousness). Thus, the only way to change your experience is by changing your consciousness. By rigidly holding onto anything in your life you keep your consciousness at the level of the thing and you stifle your growth.

The only lasting security in your life is your connection with your Inner-Self, which is where your life merges with the Divine. This is the place of unlimited possibility and from that place you create everything that is necessary in your life. So, you see there can never be any lasting security in material things because they are always changing. Your connection with the Divine is eternal and is always ready to meet you at your place of need, and that is where your security is.

Practice daily the following in your quiet time.

- Give thanks for all you have and release all you have to the Divine. Know that if something is lost in your life a way is always opened for something greater to appear. When you are thankful, the Universe will bring more things in your life to be thankful for.

- Know that the Divine always provides for your every need, but It can only give you what you are conscious of receiving.

- Know that there is unlimited possibility in uncertainty and non-attachment and this is where your security lies.

The Law of Unconditional Love and Trust

This law says that there is a Loving Divine Presence at the core of your life that created you for a purpose, and loves you beyond human comprehension. You were born with a gift, something you can do in a special way that no one else can do. When you trust in the Divine completely to unfold, this talent in your life will be supported and your every need will be met easily and harmoniously.

The Law of Unconditional Love and Trust supersedes all the other spiritual laws for it rests in the energy of Unconditional Love which is the highest energy there is. Nothing is greater than the Divine's unconditional love for Its creation and you are the Divine's creation. When you become conscious of this truth you know that all things are possible, for you realize that there is nothing that Divine Love cannot overcome.

The Divine wants you to be healthy, happy, and fulfilled, and in order to realize this in your life you must come to an understanding that you are the Divine expressing Itself as you. You are united with the Divine and all of creation. Nothing can dissolve this union. When you are conscious of this all things take their proper place in your life. The Divine is always working for good on your behalf but you must be open to receive this goodness in your life. This is the point of trust. If you could come to a place of complete trust in the Divine for your every need, your life would flow easily and harmoniously with very little stress and strain. You would have no thought of how your needs would be met tomorrow and you could live fully each day completely pouring yourself into your life's purpose. How good would it feel not to worry about the future and know that all your future needs would be met? How much anxiety and stress would be alleviated from your life if you could live each day fully knowing that you would always have enough for all your tomorrows? Trusting in the Divine's unconditional love for you is where you will find this.

For example, have you ever had a time in your life when you thought that a certain situation was horrible, and you did not understand why it was all happening to you? Yet over time that horrible situation seemed to open a door you never thought of, or you learned something invaluable. Trust is the key. That is why any circumstance, either good or bad, doesn't seem to stress people who understand the universe. They know that at the end of the day, it is for your highest good. Just imagine how your day flows so much better just knowing this information. For instance if you have a flat tire on the road, you can either be very frustrated about it or you can tell yourself that maybe it saved you from an accident ahead. That is how you change your state of being.

The Divine created you to express Itself in and through your life. It knows how and will provide for your every need but in order to do so you must trust in the Divine COMPLETELY. The problem is most people don't trust in the Divine to meet their daily needs. Instead of letting their Divine gift unfold in their lives, they seek things they think will satisfy their needs, but once accomplished they are not fulfilled. That unfulfilled feeling is always your soul seeking its true purpose.

Through the Law of Cause and Effect mentioned previously, the Divine has given you the power to create anything in your life you desire. Thus, using this law intelligently to create what you want in life is the beginning of taking charge of your life. However, most people are not fulfilled by the things they manifest in their lives because they think that material things can satisfy their desires.

Real lasting satisfaction in your life can only come in fulfilling the purpose for which you were created. As I mentioned earlier, the Divine made you to express Itself in and through your life. You have a Divine seed planted within you that is begging to be born and this is your life's purpose. You can only bring this seed to fruition through trusting the Divine and letting It govern, guard, and guide you daily.

How do I know my life's purpose, you ask? You can only find your life's purpose by surrendering your personal will to Divine will. This is done by earnestly seeking Divine guidance in your life daily.

For example, in my senior year of high school when I was trying to decide what I wanted to do in life I would comb through the jobs in the classified section of the newspapers to see how much money each job offered. I saw that engineering paid some of the highest salaries, so that's the career path I pursued and became a mechanical engineer.

However, my passion had always been in health and fitness. My cousin and I made a workout room in one of the storage barns we had on the farm when I was about 14 years old. I read everything I could get my hands on about working out, and I was really good at it. The first thing that I bought for myself after I started working in the corporate world was a membership to the local YMCA where I thoroughly enjoyed exercising.

I spent 16 years in the corporate world feeling unfulfilled before I gathered the courage to pursue my passion of health and fitness to become a personal trainer. My family and others thought I had lost my mind by leaving such a stable and well-paying job. But I knew fitness was my passion and my Divine gift so I trusted and took a leap of faith.

I've been in the personal training industry for over 20 years now and I realize that taking that leap of faith was the best thing I ever did. I have a great client base, I've written and published books on health and fitness, and most importantly, I have found that the Divine will always support me when I trust and follow Its guide.

Heaven is not some place in the sky you go to when you die. Heaven is a state of consciousness of your unity with the Divine. When you are in this state of consciousness you can materialize heavenly things right here on earth. In your unity with the Divine you have access to all that you will ever need in life. For the much sought-after Kingdom of God is a state of consciousness of the Presence of God. When realized, all your needs are met easily and harmoniously.

3 MENTAL ENERGY

*A fundamental conclusion of the new physics also acknowledges that the observer creates the reality. As observers, we are personally involved with the creation of our own reality. Physicists are being forced to admit that the universe is a "mental" construction. Pioneering physicist Sir James Jeans wrote: "The stream of knowledge is heading toward a non-mechanical reality; the universe begins to look more like a great thought than like a great machine. Mind no longer appears to be an accidental intruder into the realm of matter; we ought to rather hail it as the creator and governor of the realm of matter. Get over it, and accept the inarguable conclusion. The universe is immaterial-mental and spiritual. (**R.C. Henry**, The Mental Universe)*

Out of your mental world of thought is born the conditions and circumstances that populate your life. Entry to the spiritual realm of harmonious living can only be attained through conscious control of your thoughts. Until you realize that thoughts are what you give life to, you will live under the false idea that you are a victim of circumstance with very little control over what happens in your life.

To master your mental plane of existence is to gain control over the circumstances and conditions of your life. In order to master your mind you have to realize three very important things. First, you are the thinker before the thought, and thus, you are the gatekeeper to the thoughts you allow to enter and dwell in your mind. Second, you are a creative being and you are always creating something via the thoughts you allow to take root in your mind. Third, you are never and have never been a victim of any circumstance or condition in your life.

You Are the Thinker

This is the first truth you must realize in your quest to control your mind. Most people feel powerless as to the thoughts they entertain. However, you are the thinker before the thought and you have the power to scan every thought and choose whether or not you will allow it into your mind. In other words, you are the gatekeeper to you mind and thus you choose which thoughts you let in and which thoughts you keep out.

This is not an easy task, but it is necessary if you want to change your life. Not only are you the gatekeeper for the thoughts you allow in your mind, you have to examine your mind for the false ideas that have already taken root and are producing fruit in your life now. Some of these false ideas you got from your parents, grandparents, and other loved ones who taught you the things about life they learned. While well-meaning, some of the things they taught you may now be causing some of your biggest limitations in life. These ideas are hard to let go of because you have trusted and believed them to be true for so long.

If you are having any recurring problems or conditions you can't seem to overcome it may be that you have a deep-rooted belief that you are unconsciously aware of in your mental garden. This belief was probably planted in your childhood by some well-meaning people in your life, or it could be a result of some deep hurt you have experienced. However, you must get rid of this false idea if you are to change the condition. For example, when I was a child my older brother was very outgoing and I was completely the opposite. Consequently, my brother got all the attention at my expense and I was deeply hurt. As a result, I learned to guard my heart and not to let people get very close to me. This belief carried over into my relationships as an adult and I could never let anyone get really close to me no matter how hard I tried. It wasn't until I realized that subconsciously I was still carrying the same belief from my childhood that I could change my relationships. I had to uproot that old belief before I could let people get close to me again.

You also allow false ideas to subconsciously enter your mind through conversation with friends, things you read, and what you hear in the news. You have to be vigilant of what you consciously allow to be planted in your mental garden, for a thought will always produce fruit in the form of conditions after its kind.

You are a Creative Being

You are always creating the circumstances and conditions of your life via your thoughts and beliefs. What you believe to be true will always manifest in your life as a condition or circumstance. Behind every condition and circumstance in your life is an underlying thought and belief. If you want to know the sum total of your thoughts and beliefs, just look at the conditions and circumstances presently in your life. This is a very sobering exercise, but you must accept it if you want to create the life that you desire.

As previously mentioned, thoughts are things and when you give a thought your attention you give it energy by allowing it to be planted in your mind. The more attention you give the thought the more you nurture and energize it until it becomes a belief and blossoms into a condition in your life. You are always thinking, and thus, always creating something and herein lies the problems and the solutions in your life.

Most people allow their minds to aimlessly wander and so they allow random thoughts to be planted in their mental garden. Some of these thoughts are constructive and they bloom into constructive conditions, while others are destructive and they blossom into undesirable conditions. Consequently, most people believe the conditions and circumstances of their lives just randomly happen. They get some things that they want and other things they don't want.

Look at it like this, you are the architect of your life and the thoughts you allow to take root in your mind are the blueprint by which your life is built. If you don't like the house you built you can remodel it or completely tear it down and build one you like but, you can only do this by changing your thoughts.

You Are Not a Victim of Circumstance

If you have read this far you now realize that you are not and never have been a victim of circumstance. No circumstance or condition can ever hold you powerless because you created the circumstance or condition through the thoughts you allowed to germinate in your mental garden. You can pluck out the condition causing thoughts from your mental garden just as easily you would pull weeds out of a physical garden.

You have the inner power to create the life of your dreams. The key to accessing this power is mastery of your mental activity. Always remember you are the thinker before the thought and thus the gatekeeper of the thoughts you allow to be planted in your mental garden.

4 HEALING MODALITIES

My name is Alisha Lalji. I was born in Canada, but spent the majority of my youth living in the United States. You could say I have led an abnormal life compared to most. Much of my life was shrouded in secrecy and I was forced to adopt dual identities at an early age. Close friends would tell me my story was shocking and belonged in a movie or novel.

Not only did I experience a unique and at times very troubling life, but I dealt with the everyday stresses and challenges the majority of us face. An awkward upbringing, low self-esteem, battling addictions, continually moving homes and schools, feeling rejected by my own culture, illness, financial challenges, and weight issues were some of the difficulties I faced all the time. I felt like a victim because of my life circumstances and thought I was powerless to change. This was the hand life had dealt me; this was my destiny.

I felt like I was seeing the world as an adult through a child's body. I was an observer to my own life, unable to fit in with normality. I would deeply feel the traumas in my life, other people's lives, animals around me, and humanity at large. The more I grappled with accepting this, the more questions arose within me.

Why is the world this way? I would repeatedly ask. What did an innocent child like me do to deserve this life? I was trying so hard but life kept knocking me back down. I should just quit and give up was a thought that perpetually looped in my head. I was in a dark space surrounded by self-pity when one day a friend jarred me free from feeling sorry for myself. From that day forth I felt I could leave my victim mindset behind and begin changing my life.

I have spent most of my life interested in stories of people's transformative journeys from having nothing to everything they desired. How did they manage to do it? Was there a secret to how life worked that I was unaware of? The more I delved for answers the more questions came to mind. Who is God or this universal Life Force I keep hearing about? Doesn't God love all of us? If so, then why is the world in such a condition? Why am I here on Earth and what is my purpose?

In my quest of pursuing answers to life's questions, the universe led me on a transformative journey of the skin, body, mind, spirit, and soul. This journey liberated me, dramatically shifted my perspective on life, aligned me to meet the life partner of my dreams, and taught me to be happy no matter what the circumstances are in my life. Along my journey I was fortunate to explore several different healing modalities and techniques that accelerated my transformation and I would like to share them with you.

Skin

Beauty is not in the face; beauty is a light in the heart. (**Kahlil Gibran**, *artist, poet, and writer*)

During my childhood and teenage years I dealt with severe acne and very sensitive skin. I went to a series of dermatologists for years and tried every harsh medication on the market. My self-esteem plummeted due to being teased repeatedly about my appearance. This motivated me to embark on a journey of acquiring in-depth knowledge of the skin through aesthetics and working with a dermatologist and plastic surgeon. Later I went on to create a **Facial** combining treatments which infused traditional techniques, natural ingredients, and modern technology to treat the skin not just on the outer layer, but also on a dermal, muscular, and even cellular level. This treatment fixed severe acne in minimal time, and eliminated wrinkles permanently without the need for surgery or any recovery time. It felt incredible to help clients who couldn't face looking in the mirror and felt unattractive in their own skin, just as I had.

I knew the importance of caring for my face, but I realized I was missing something for my body. The skin is the largest organ in the body and is responsible for one quarter of the detoxification we go through every day. While learning the ancient Indian practice of **Ayurveda,** I came across a technique used to detoxify our lymphatic system, exfoliate the body, and increase circulation and energy called **Dry Brushing**. I recommend using a dry brush for a few minutes daily. Brushing over the entire body after showering or bathing will yield the best results.

The problem with my skin was not fixed yet. I still had to figure out how to deal with the dryness and irritation I was experiencing. Parts of my skin would itch and become irritated to the point where they would bleed and eventually scar. What was causing my skin to react this way? It must be something external irritating my skin. What was I putting on my skin to cause this irritation?

I later learned that it only takes 26 seconds for chemicals placed on the skin to enter the bloodstream. While discovering what ingredients were in my hair, body, and face products, I came to a shocking realization… all of my products were filled with chemicals, chemicals, and more chemicals! Not surprisingly my skin was reacting terribly. This realization got me into **Aromatherapy** which is an alternative medicine utilizing plants and aromatic plant oils including essential oils to heal the skin, body, mind, and spirit. Now all my products are made from natural and potent essential oils instead of harsh chemicals. My growing love of essential oils didn't stop there. Soon I was using essential oils for everything including common colds, digestive problems, mosquito repellent, mind clearing, and energizing my body.

Body

Take care of your body. It's the only place you have to live in. (***Jim Rohn***, *entrepreneur, author and motivational speaker*)

Life took an unexpected turn when I found myself back in my birthplace of Vancouver, Canada, in my mid-twenties. What a big climate shift coming from sunny California to rainy Vancouver. Even though I had spent some of my early childhood years in Vancouver, I felt like a bit of an outsider. If dealing with the mental stress of re-assimilating to my home country, being unable to return to California to even say goodbye to those I was close to, and restarting my career wasn't hard enough, I was also experiencing severe physical pain and was in need of surgery. The pain became so intense that even tripling the recommended dose of extra strength pain medication failed to alleviate my symptoms. I underwent surgery to remove my gallbladder and deep down I knew it was because of stress. What was happening to me? Was I damaging my health and causing this sickness? One thing I knew for certain was that I needed to make some changes.

During my illness a desire was sparked within me to truly understand the body. This led me to the study of holistic, energy-based, and non-traditional methods for healing the body. Around this time a serendipitous moment, which I later viewed as a universal synchronicity introduced me to my life partner, Tom Partridge. He was supportive of my quest to heal, delve into the self, and discover true happiness in life.

I began to study **Massage** incorporating healing modalities such as **Swedish, Deep Tissue, Reflexology, Joint Release, Deep Flow, Shiatsu**, and **Sports Massage**. I started seeing the physical changes in my body and the pain dissipated. Previously my view of massage had been one of pampering; now I realized the healing importance of massage for health and vitality in the body. While treating clients with physical pain through massage it became clear that some knots in the body did not want to release. What was it that was preventing this release?

Through much in-depth scientific research I began to wrap my head around the idea that we are all energy beings. This seemed to resonate with the knots not wanting to release in the human body. It made sense that these knots were energetic blockages within the body and they would not release until the emotion within was processed. This path led me to study the ancient practice of **Reiki**. In the art of Reiki the practitioner is a conduit for channeling life energy and releasing blocks in the body, mind and spirit. I was introduced to the seven **Chakras** and how these energetic centers relate to a different aspect of the body and self. If there are blocks in any one of the seven chakras it can lead to illness and disease.

I learned that not only are there seven chakras in the body, but there are also seven **Earth Chakras** that each correspond to the chakras in our own body. Not only does the Earth have chakras it also has **Vortexes**. You can think of chakras as energetic inflows and vortexes as energetic outflows of the planet. My partner and I visited the first chakra of the planet at Mount Shasta, California, as well as a powerful planetary vortex in Sedona, Arizona. It is incredible how quickly blocks in the mind, body, and spirit are released in these locations. We could feel the energetic differences in these hot spots and understood why people traveled from around the world to heal at these places.

Integrating the realization that we are all energy beings changed my perspective on everything. I found out that **Muscle Testing** is a way of evaluating the body's imbalances and instantly assessing its needs. Muscle testing is a tool that provides valuable information on energy blockages, nutritional deficiencies, food sensitivities, and much more. This technique is used by naturopaths, but you can also learn to self-muscle test. Once proficient, I could check whether the food I was about to eat resonated with me energetically. In my excitement not only was I utilizing muscle testing for food choices, but for all parts of my life including the mystical and once unimaginable aspects.

Crystals opened my eyes to a different world of healing. There are countless crystals and stones that aid in healing all sorts of ailments for the skin, body, mind, and spirit. I wore certain crystals as pendants to aid in my migraines, digestion, focus, and spiritual expansion. I aligned chakra stones under my bed to sync with my body's chakras while I slept.

Cranial Sacral is another healing method that focuses on the bones in the head, spinal column, and sacrum. The purpose of this non-invasive therapy is to bring the body into alignment through releasing skeletal compression, alleviating stress, and pain.

I found using a **Foot Detox** machine on a regular basis was the best way of eliminating the toxins accumulating in my body. For most of us we intake more toxins than our bodies can eliminate which is why regular detoxification treatments are so important. A foot detox session usually begins with placing the feet in a warm salt water bath. Through the process of ionization, objects and different colors form in the water revealing which organ in the body the toxicity is coming from.

Mind

We cannot solve our problems with the same thinking we used when we created them.
(**Albert Einstein**, *theoretical physicist and philosopher of science*)

As my healing skills progressed I was able to see rapid transformation in my clients. But despite my success, I still felt like I was missing something. We are all energy beings and the blocks or knots stored in our bodies have both energetic and physical components to them. I wondered from an energetic perspective what were my blocks and was it necessary to delve into them before a release could take place? These blocks were emotional holds, generally a fear, a suppressed experience, or some type of trauma. Not every block requires mental exploration in order to release it, but it certainly helps greatly with the larger and more painful blocks in the body and mind. By healing the mental components of these blocks I began to understand that our mind and thoughts shape our experiences and affect our physical reality.

It was a difficult idea to accept initially. The concept of my thoughts literally creating the world around me seemed very surreal. I took a step back and examined my life and despite my progression in healing myself and others, I was still unhappy with my life and circumstances. To fully accept that my thoughts were creating my reality I had to come to terms with the fact that the negativity in my life was my own doing. My thoughts had generated the good and the bad in my life. This was very difficult to accept, but once I fully embraced it, I felt incredibly liberated. I had found the key to changing my life and it seemed so simple.

All I needed to do was to change my thoughts and patterns quickly. I needed to broaden my understanding of the mind. I delved into studying the subconscious, the part of our minds that controls 95 percent of our emotions, self-esteem, beliefs, immune system, and body. The question arose of how to change a thought pattern when we predominantly use our conscious mind which equates to only 5 percent of our entire mind. I knew that it took three weeks to change a habit, but now it made perfect sense that that was how long it took to build new neural pathways in the brain, which in turn would affect the subconscious.

Through the art of **Hypnotherapy** I could go directly into the subconscious mind and see the origin of specific behaviors, patterns, and traumas in both the body and mind. Through studying hypnotherapy, a form of psychotherapy, I learned how detrimental television and certain genres of music can be in negatively programming the subconscious. I reduced and eventually stopped watching television, and changed my music playlists to more positive, instrumental, and uplifting tones. I noticed a big difference in the way I felt by doing this and I cannot overemphasize the importance of reducing or eliminating your time in front of the television! I now had all the tools and motivation I needed to release internal blockages and create the lasting changes I deeply desired.

In my continued pursuit of understanding the subconscious mind's relationship to the body I came across a modality called **Somatic Healing**. With somatic healing the subconscious drives movements in the body to unwind physical traumas and eliminate pain. This technique can be used for a variety of ailments including injuries, stress-related pain, arthritis, fibromyalgia, and sciatica. I was able to unwind accidents my client had experienced and release the injury from a cellular level, promoting fast and easy healing in the body and mind.

I now had a strong understanding of the subconscious. I was in a state of flow in finding out who I truly was, and now could begin peeling away the mental layers to reveal my true self. My clients could now release past traumas of abuse, neglect, and fear. It was a privilege to see the power and speed of the transformation my clients were experiencing.

To take my clients even deeper into the subconscious mind, I began to incorporate **Sound Healing**, which is used by many ancient cultures as a powerful healing tool for the body, mind, spirit, and soul. Sound healing is used in music, ancient chanting, Tibetan singing bowls, bells, tuning forks, and many other applications. I use the love healing frequency of 528 Hz in my treatments. This specific frequency has proven to even heal damaged DNA. Nikola Tesla said, "If you wish to understand the Universe think of energy, frequency, and vibration."

Spirit-Soul

Until you make the unconscious conscious, it will direct your life and you will call it fate.
(Carl Jung, *psychiatrist and psychotherapist)*

All seemed to be heading in the right direction in my healing journey. I had all the tools I felt I needed to manifest what I desired. Despite all of this, things still were not flowing the way I had expected. I felt like I was swimming against the current of a river. Things seemed harder than they needed to be. Again, I felt like something was missing. It was at this time the universe was showing many signs and synchronicities to both my partner and I. This seemed very surreal at first, but through all of this I saw what I was missing...the magic of spirit-soul.

Everywhere I journeyed I repeatedly saw the word **Alchemy**. The common perception of alchemy is transforming lead into gold. The ancient alchemists wrote that the core of their transformation was the human soul. Their goal was transmuting the base metals of human emotion into the gold of self-realization.

The study of alchemy opened my mind more than any other area. I finally saw the immense power of the subconscious. I now understood that it was a gateway to the inner soul and the universe. Infinite knowledge was accessible through the subconscious. The great spiritual teachers have taught the importance of going inwards. I finally understood that reality was an internally generated mechanism and how journeying inward aligns all that we are and all that we desire.

In the magical and wonderful realm of the subconscious I was able to access past lives, repressed memories, and much more. It was a profound realization to connect with angelic beings, spirit guides, and inner healers for the first time in this realm. I felt loved in a way that is indescribable. I knew no matter what I was never alone. It was such an uplifting feeling to know that I had guidance in all aspects of my life.

I began to deeply reflect on all the aspects of my past that no longer served me. I realized that these negative traits were a part of societal conditioning and programming. No wonder I had felt like I was swimming against the current. I had learned an important lesson: in order to utilize the concept of thoughts creating reality for your betterment, those thoughts must be aligned with the inner you—what some would call your higher self. It was in embracing this idea that allowed my career path to do a complete 180 degree turn.

Daily **Meditation** helped align me with my higher self. I soon realized that meditation was the big missing piece and the top down approach to true happiness. I repeat a mantra during my meditation and feel a great sense of connectedness with all that is. I feel a great release, a profound sense of inner peace, and inspiration flowing through me in a beautiful state of silence.

I am now completely FREE! Free of fear, free of stress, and free of hatred. These dark emotions have been replaced with joy, love, and happiness. Things now flow and make sense without my rational mind understanding how. I feel divinely guided by a universal intelligence and life has never been more magical. I do not have to think, as I am guided by synchronicities each and every step of the way. I know infinite knowledge exists within me and above all else I can now say I truly feel happy.

Alchemy Theta Therapies

Let yourself be silently drawn by the strange pull of what you really love. It will not lead you astray. (**Rumi**, *poet, scholar, and mystic*)

As our healing toolbox continued to grow, my partner and I became fascinated with this newfound knowledge of alchemy, the subconscious mind, and meditation. Transformative exploration through the subconscious mind has been used for thousands of years by yogis, shamans, and monks. We all tap into our subconscious mind through lucid dreaming or REM sleep, also referred to as the Theta brainwave state. We can also access the subconscious through deep meditation and hypnosis.

My partner and I both wanted to know how we could incorporate the Theta brainwave state used for accessing the subconscious into the modalities and healing techniques we knew for optimal transformation. We wanted an easy way for people to experience the Theta state as the majority of clients had not consciously experienced it before. This is when **Alchemy Theta Therapies** came to light. We would guide clients on an inward journey into the body and mind through exploration of the senses via deep relaxation. The relaxation experienced was unlike anything else. While in this state it was as if a story was unfolding before you as you journeyed into yourself. The clients only needed to relax and enjoy the blissful and euphoric experience of integrating all of the senses.

As Alchemy Theta Therapies grew and evolved we worked hard to integrate alchemy, science, wellness, and healing into the different modalities. The effects of massage were blended with the limitless potential of the Theta state to create **Alchemy Theta Massage**. Within this relaxing treatment the body and mind are able to release knots, blocks, tension, and pain easily and effortlessly.

Through my extensive experience of treating the skin and my knowledge of the subconscious mind, I created a revolutionary method for reversing the effects of aging quickly and effectively. I named this method **Alchemy Theta Facial**. While receiving a facial, clients are guided on an inward journey exploring the fountain of youth and utilizing specific formulas to activate elastin, collagen, and the metabolism on a cellular level.

We were very fortunate to offer these therapies to clients and the media while receiving recognition in international publications. Our desire was to share these therapies to the wellness industry at large, but we felt that an expansion of our Alchemy Theta Treatments was necessary to address additional problems the general populous faced.

A major health concern in today's world is obesity, especially in North America. I dealt with a myriad of weight issues and yo-yoed with a variety of diets and techniques for over a decade. The current state of the food industry with the number of additives, chemicals, antibiotics, genetic modification, and industrial factory farming certainly didn't make losing weight any easier. My shock with aspects of the food industry led me to change to an organic Pescetarian diet high in alkaline foods. I still knew there was more to weight loss than I had first realized. Subconscious blocks were a big part of it and I had experienced many of these blocks. A side of my psyche wanted to repeatedly quit before I gained any real momentum, due to the number times I had failed in the past. In tackling these subconscious blocks directly we came up with **Alchemy Theta Slimming**. This is a top down approach to addressing weight loss through the mind. With this treatment the metabolism is activated and the desire to eat healthy and to enjoy an active lifestyle is engrained deeply within.

Stress is another huge health concern for many. A large portion of illnesses are due to stress and toxicity in the body and mind. Through an energetic understanding of the body and mind we were able to create an **Alchemy Theta Body & Mind Detox** treatment. This consists of an introspective journey in which clients go through mental exercises to release stress, negative feelings, and unwanted thoughts and emotions. Clients are left feeling lighter, and more vibrant, rejuvenated, balanced, and calm.

For clients ready for deeper healing of the body, mind, and spirit, we created **Alchemy Theta Chakra Balancing**. In this treatment we align all seven chakras of the body through the use of Reiki and healing stones that connect specifically to each chakra center. Clients feel the release and activation of each chakra and are left with a profound sense of peace, revitalization, and energetic balance.

My partner and I both feel very fortunate to recommend these five therapies that incorporate a powerful mix of modalities and techniques such as massage, facials, Reiki, healing crystals, sound healing, and much more. I know the universe has taken us on this journey and to this point in our understanding in order to create these healing treatments. We leave it in the hands of the universe to see where it takes us. We hope that many may be able to experience the wonders of these healing treatments, and those who do are nudged toward an inner awakening with the ability to change any aspect of their lives they desire.

Conclusion

I thank the universe for putting me on an incredible journey of healing myself, discovering who I truly am, and seeing my inner truth. I know my path is far from complete and I view the journey itself as more important than the destination. I have adopted a continuous change mentality toward my life and know that there is so much more growth, lessons, and experiences ahead of me. Paradoxically I now realize that the more I know, the more I am aware of just how much I don't know, and how much is out there still waiting to be discovered and explored.

The driving engine behind my transformation was my quest to understand the relationship between our intentions and the universe at large. When you align your dreams with specificity and intention to the universe, the universe cannot do anything but bring those dreams and goals to fruition. The universe acts like a giant mirror reflecting your inner thoughts back to you through physical reality. The physics behind manifestation are not fundamentally complex. Always remember that your dreams must be in integrity, aligned with your inner self, and that you must not hold expectations on the final outcome. The universe can bring to you things far beyond the limits of what you can imagine, so do not try to limit the outcome or parameters of your dreams. Just go with the flow in life, dream your dream, and see how life transforms in front of you in an explosion of synchronicity and signs guiding you to a place beyond your wildest dreams.

Imagine taking introspection one step further. Do you want to change the world for the better with minimal external effort? How quickly Earth would change if every human projected thoughts of peace, abundance, healing, and happiness. What if people stopped focusing on war, hunger, fear, violence, and poverty and thus stopped perpetuating these events through the power of their thoughts? Did you know by actually watching negative news you are perpetuating more of that fear, war, and poverty into the world? What if instead we lived an existence of love, light, and joy by thinking, feeling, and seeing more of that positivity? If this sounds far-fetched you may be surprised to know that it does not take too many in this space of love and joy to positively impact humanity.

When I connected to spirit my life changed dramatically, and if I could do it all over again I would have opened up my spiritual awareness and meditative practices years ago. Connecting with spirit provides a truly top down approach to life changes. I believed, I let go, I connected to the all-knowing space deep within my heart, and knew without a doubt that everything happening in my life was for a higher purpose. I am truly happy and know that my external circumstances really do not matter. I am grateful for my life circumstances, lessons, and hardships as I know that if I had not ventured into the dark I would not have seen the light of self-realization. I feel very blessed to be doing what I love in life, sharing my knowledge and healing skills with others, and above all experiencing it with the love of my life, Tom Partridge.

Tips: Picking The Healing Modality For You

Choose a healing modality that you truly believe in and that resonates with you as only then will you be open to experience it fully.

Most of the time you will feel a little worse before you feel better. For instance, your body might be sore immediately after a massage but later will feel amazing. A release of toxins from the body may cause a headache or fatigue. Understand that this is all part of the healing process, and that experiencing these symptoms does not mean the modality was ineffective; it is actually quite the opposite.

Pick something you are committed to working on and be patient as changes, especially big ones, may take some time.

Remember to dream your dream, but at the end of the day it is all about taking those baby steps. Feeling good and baby-stepping toward your goals and desires will be a fun and pressure-free recipe for success.

Make sure to pat yourself on the back for all your little changes and improvements. Being hard on yourself is the last thing you want to do. Remember when you are grateful for the little changes, the universe in its reflective nature and infinite wisdom will bring you more changes for you to be happy and grateful for.

Choose the healing modality that excites you the most, drop any expectations, and have fun!

5 PHYSICAL ENERGY

Starting your daily activity in your spiritual energy, then mastering your mental energy allows a harmonious flow of energy into your physical activities. Your physical body is the end result of the creative flow of energy from spirit into matter.

Your body is designed by the Divine for movement. It is a magnificently designed living organism and, if properly taken care of, will provide you health, strength, and mobility for all of your years here on earth.

Think of it like this, your body is the only vehicle you have through which you can do your daily activities. There are two very important components to maintaining a healthy body: daily exercise and proper nutrition.

People seem to think that once they reach the age of forty, their bodies start to deteriorate, slipping down the slope into "old" age. They blame their lack of energy, their pudgy appearance, and their aches and pains on "getting old." Most of these symptoms are however the result of years of negative thinking, lack of exercise, and poor dietary choices. The key to keeping your body fit and firm as you age is making healthy lifestyle choices on a daily basis.

It's a proven fact that people who make healthy lifestyle choices live longer and have a better quality of life than those who adopt unhealthy habits. So, deciding to incorporate healthy habits into your life is the first step to getting and staying fit and firm with age. The next step is choosing those activities that are the most beneficial in your quest to stay fit and firm.

Those, including myself, who stay fit and firm as the years pass find that a positive state of mind, and a proper mix of strength training, cardiovascular exercise, and balanced nutrition is fundamental to getting and staying healthy as you mature. Al Beckles and the late Jack LaLanne can teach us so much about living a healthy lifestyle.

Al Beckles is a legend in the bodybuilding world. At the age of 55, Al placed second in the Mr. Olympia competition, the premier bodybuilding event which thousands of competitors from across the world dream of winning each year. Al Beckles competed into his sixties because his physique was still phenomenal and better than competitors more than half his age

Jack LaLanne was a living icon to the benefits of healthy thinking, eating, and exercise. Over the years he performed amazing feats of strength and conditioning on his birthday. Jack worked out well into his 90s, devoting one and a half hours each day to strength training. This is a true testament to the value of strength training as you mature.

While I don't place myself in the same class with Jack LaLanne and Al Beckles I can tell you the value that healthy lifestyle habits have in my life. I am in my fifties and I keep my body fat at 10 percent or less. My fitness program consists of four strength training sessions each week followed by 20 minutes of cardio. I can chest press 100 pound dumbbells for 10 repetitions and leg press more than 1000 pounds, neither of which I could do in my twenties.

Exercise

Strength training and cardiovascular exercise is the foundation of your physical fitness program. Strength training builds and maintains healthy muscle mass, and cardiovascular exercise strengthens your heart and lungs.

Strength Training

As you age strength training is the best thing you can do to improve your health and fitness level. Strength training is important because around age 40 you start to experience muscle loss. "If you don't do anything to replace the lean muscle you lose, you'll increase the percentage of fat in your body," says Dr. Edward Laskowski, a physical medicine and rehabilitation specialist at the Mayo Clinic in Rochester, Minnesota. Left unabated, you can lose up to 10 pounds of muscle each decade starting at age 40.

Losing muscle is detrimental to your fitness because muscle is the component of your body that burns the majority of the calories you consume each day. Therefore, when you lose muscle your body requires fewer calories to function. Consequently, those extra calories you consume are stored as fat around your waist, hips, and other places.

Your body constantly burns calories, even when doing nothing. This resting metabolic rate is much higher in people with more muscle. Every pound of muscle uses about six calories a day to sustain itself, while each pound of fat burns only two calories daily. This small difference can add up over time. In addition, after a bout of resistance training, muscles are activated all over your body, increasing your average daily metabolic rate.

Increasing your metabolism isn't the only benefit of strength training. It also helps: [1]

- **Develop strong bones**. By stressing your bones, strength training increases bone density and reduces the risk of osteoporosis.

- **Control your weight**. As you gain muscle, your body burns calories more efficiently which can result in weight loss. The more toned your muscles, the easier it is to control your weight.

- **Reduce your risk of injury**. Building muscle protects your joints from injury. It also helps maintain flexibility and balance which are crucial to remaining independent as you age.

- **Boost your stamina**. Building muscle helps to increase your energy level while improving your sense of well-being. Strength training can boost self-confidence, improve body image, and reduce the risk of depression.

- **Sleep better**. People who strength train on a regular basis are less likely to have insomnia.

- **Manage chronic conditions**. Strength training can reduce the signs and symptoms of many chronic conditions, including arthritis, back pain, depression, diabetes, obesity, and osteoporosis.

A good strength training program should consist of exercises that target all the major muscle groups and should be performed two to four times each week. In the following pages, I've included a very good strength training routine you can do in the comfort of your home with very little equipment. You will need the following items:

- A therapeutic ball (a 65cm will generally work)
- Light, medium, and heavy resistance tubing
- An anchor for the resistance tubing that you can anchor in a closed

---

[1] MayoClinic.org

door

- A set of dumbbells consistent with your strength level

6 STRENGTH TRAINING ROUTINE

Here is a very good strength training routine you can do in the comfort of your home. I suggest you do this routine two to three times each week with at least one day of recovery between sessions.

Exercise 1: Wall Ball Squats

Start in a standing position and place a therapeutic ball at the small of your back up against a sturdy wall. Position your feet in front of you, about 2 feet from the wall, and a little wider than shoulder width. Turn your toes outward slightly. From this starting position squat until your thighs are parallel to the floor and then return to an upright position. Make sure to keep the ball pressed firmly against your back throughout the entire movement. Also, keep your chest up and your weight on your heels throughout the exercise.

Do 3 sets of 15 repetitions. You can make this exercise harder by holding a dumbbell in each hand while doing this exercise.

Areas targeted: thighs, hamstrings, and buttocks

Exercise 2: Stationary Lunges

Start in an upright position with your feet shoulder width apart. Position your hands behind your head as illustrated. Take a giant step forward and drop your hips while bending both knees until your front thigh is parallel to the floor. Return to the starting position and alternate legs.

Keep your chest up throughout this exercise and step out to where your thigh makes a 90 degree angle with your ankle.

Do 3 sets of 10 repetitions each leg

Areas targeted: thighs, buttocks, and hamstrings

Exercise 3: Hip Lifts

Lay on your back with your legs extended and your feet on the ball as illustrated. Lift your hips off the floor and pull the ball into toward your body, then extend your legs and return to the starting position and repeat. Keep your hips up off the floor during the whole exercise.

Do 3 sets of 15 repetitions

Area targeted: hamstrings, buttocks, calves, and stomach

Exercise 4: Pushups

A properly performed pushup is one of the best overall upper body strength exercises you can do. Start with your body completely extended and your hands positioned a little wider than shoulder width as illustrated. Pull your navel in, inhale and lower your body until your chest touches the floor. Exhale and push your body back up to the starting position and repeat. (Do modified pushups on your knees if you are not strong enough to do them as described above)

Do 3 sets of 10 repetitions

Areas targeted: chest, shoulders, triceps and core

Exercise 5: Bent Over Lat Pull

Anchor your medium resistance tubing head height. Stand back far enough from the anchor point to where the tubing is tight. Squat slightly and extend both arms over your head. Now, while keeping one arm totally extended, exhale and pull one hand to the side of your chest, and then return it to over your head and repeat with the other hand.

Do 3 sets of 10 repetitions each hand

Areas targeted: upper back

Exercise 6: Lateral Shoulder Raises

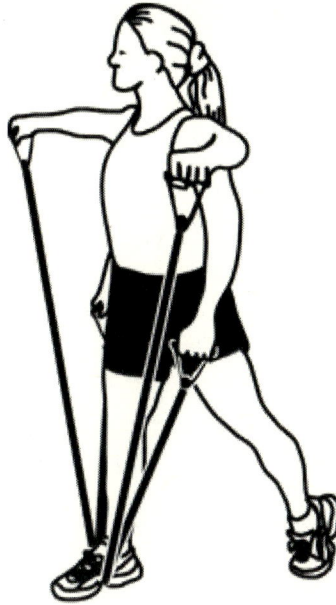

Use a light resistance tube. Position the tube under one foot as illustrated. Start with your arms at your side and lift your hands to shoulder height while keeping your arms totally extended. Your palms should be facing down at the top of this exercise. Then return your hands to your side and repeat.

Do 3 sets of 10 repetitions

Area targeted: shoulders

Exercise 7: Standing Biceps Curl

Stand with your feet shoulder width apart and your knees slightly bent as illustrated. Start with your arms totally extended by your side and then curl the dumbbells up to shoulder height. Then return to your starting position and repeat. Be sure to keep your elbows close to your body throughout this exercise.

Do 3 sets of 10 repetitions

Area targeted: biceps

Exercise 8: Over Head Triceps Extensions

Position a medium resistance band firmly under your foot as illustrated. Start with your hands behind your head and extend your arms fully until your hands are over your head. Then return to the starting position and repeat. Be sure to keep your elbows close to the side of your head throughout this exercise.

Do 3 sets of 10 repetitions

Area targeted: triceps

Exercise 9: Seated Twist

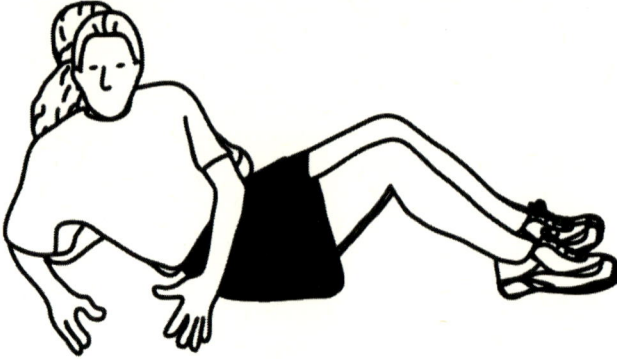

Sit on the floor with your knees slightly bent and your chest up as illustrated. Position your hands as if you were holding a small ball. Twist your upper body to one side and touch the floor with both hands and then twist to the other side. Keep your chest up and naval pulled in tightly throughout this exercise.

Do 3 sets of 15 repetitions each side

Areas targeted: stomach, obliques, and lower back

7 CARDIOVASCULAR EXERCISE

Cardiovascular exercise known as cardio by most in the fitness profession is associated with numerous health benefits; therefore, it is an invaluable part of any fitness program. Cardio exercise is any activity that increases the work of the heart and lungs. Activities such as brisk walking, running, training on the elliptical machine, biking, and working on the Stairmaster, are some of the more well-known forms of cardio.

During cardio exercise you repeatedly move large muscles in the upper and lower parts of your body. Your body responds by breathing faster and more deeply providing increased blood flow to these muscles and back to your lungs. Your small blood vessels widen to deliver more oxygen to your muscles and carry away waste products, such as carbon dioxide and lactic acid. Your body also releases endorphins which are natural pain killers that promote an increased sense of well-being.

Regardless of your age, cardio exercise is good for you. As your body adapts to a cardio routine your heart and lungs will become stronger and more efficient in performing their activities. The following are additional benefits of cardiovascular exercise:[2]

- **Helps to lose and maintain a healthy weight.** Combined with strength training and a healthy diet cardio helps you to lose weight and to keep it off.

- **Increase your stamina.** Cardio may make you tired in the short term, but over the long term, you will enjoy increased stamina and reduced fatigue.

- **Ward off viral illnesses.** Cardio activates your immune system, thus making you less susceptible to minor viral illnesses such as colds and flu.

- **Reduce health risks.** Cardio, combined with strength training, reduces the risk of many conditions including obesity, heart disease, high blood pressure, type 2 diabetes, stroke, osteoporosis, and certain types of cancer.

---

[2] MayoClinic.org

- **Manage chronic conditions.** Cardio, combined with strength training, helps to lower blood pressure and to control blood sugar.

- **Strengthen your heart.** A stronger heart doesn't need to beat as fast and pumps blood more efficiently. Consequently, blood flow is improved to all parts of your body.

- **Keeps your arteries clear.** Cardio boosts your high-density lipoprotein (HDL) or "good" cholesterol and lowers your low-density lipoprotein (LDL) or "bad" cholesterol, which results in less plaque build-up in your arteries.

- **Boost your mood.** Cardio can ease the gloominess of depression, reduce the tension associated with anxiety and promote relaxation.

- **Stay active and independent as you get older.** Cardio, in conjunction with strength training, keeps your muscles strong, helping you maintain mobility as you get older. Cardio also keeps your mind sharp. At least 30 minutes of cardio three days a week seems to reduce cognitive decline in older adults.

Now that you know cardiovascular exercise is good for you, let's discuss a program that will get you the best results. A brief explanation of how your body responds to exercise will help you understand how to do your cardio in a manner that is most efficient in helping you burn body fat and firm-up. Your body has two basic ways of generating energy for your muscles in response to exercise. One involves your body using oxygen to burn calories to provide fuel to exercising muscles. In this method, your body is most efficient in burning stored body fat because fat must have oxygen present to be converted into energy to fuel your muscles. Activities that cause your body to use this method to generate energy are called aerobic. Examples are brisk walking and slow running. When you are doing activities such as these, you are exercising in the aerobic zone.

The other method that your body uses to provides fuel to muscles does not require the use of oxygen. In this method your body primarily uses carbohydrates that are stored in the muscle to generate energy. Anaerobic activities that require a quick burst of energy such as heavy weight lifting and sprinting require your body to use this method. Activities that cause your body to use this energy production system are called anaerobic exercises.

Knowing which energy system you are using when you exercise is important if you want to maximize fat burning. In my fitness program, I do strength training in the anaerobic zone to build and maintain muscle, while performing cardio in the aerobic zone to burn fat.

When planning your cardio exercise program, design it around the following three concepts:

Frequency – I recommend you do at least three sessions of cardio each week but no more than six. This is ample exercise to achieve the health benefit, and burn body fat, while also giving your body maximum recovery time to build and maintain your hard earned muscle mass. I personally do four to five cardio sessions per week as a part of my fitness program.

Intensity – I suggest you do your cardio exercise in the range of 60 to 80 percent of your estimated maximum heart rate. This is called your aerobic zone and is where your body is most efficient at burning fat as fuel. Anything above 80 percent of your estimated maximum heart rate will tap into your anaerobic energy production system, meaning you will stop using stored body fat to feed your muscles.

Use the following method to calculate your estimated maximum heart rate and your aerobic exercise zone. Take the number 220 and subtract your age. This is your estimated maximum heart rate. Now take 60 percent of this number to get the lower end of the range of your aerobic zone and 80 percent of this number to get the upper end.

For example, I am 55 years old, so my estimated maximum heart rate is 220 – 55 = 165 beats per minute (bpm). Therefore, the lower end of the range of my aerobic zone is 165 bpm x 60% = 99 bpm, and the upper end of my aerobic zone is 169 bpm x 80% = 132 bpm. So when I do my cardio exercise, I work out at a heart rate between 99 to 132 bpm.

The easiest way to see if you are staying in your aerobic zone is with a heart rate monitor. If you do not have access to a heart rate monitor, you can use the following method to check your heart rate and stay in your aerobic zone. Take the lower and upper range numbers you calculated above and divide them by four. This is your 15 second heart rate count. Then during your workout periodically stop and check your pulse for 15 seconds to see if your heart rate falls between the two numbers you just calculated.

I'll use my example again. The lower and upper ends of the range of my aerobic zone are 99 and 132 bpm, respectively. Therefore, my 15 second heart rate count is 99 bpm / 4 = 25 for the lower end of the range and 132 / 4 = 33 for the upper end. Thus, when I'm doing cardio, I stop to check my pulse for 15 seconds making sure the number I get is between 25 and 33, so I'm in my aerobic exercise zone. This is the intensity range that my body is most efficient at burning fat for fuel to provide my muscles the energy to exercise.

Duration – It is my observation that you get the most benefit from your cardio program if you combine it with strength training and do between 30 and 45 minutes three to six days each week. Do the 30 minute sessions after strength training and the 45 minute sessions on the days that you do not weight lift.

Design your cardio exercise program around the three principles above and you'll notice a real difference in the way you look and feel.

8 NUTRITION

I have to be honest and tell you that more than 75 percent of the exercise required to stay fit and firm as you age involves a fork and knife. No amount of exercise can compensate for poor dietary habits. I believe in finding a healthy eating plan that works for you, and one you can live with for the long-term.

Fad diets don't work because they are too restrictive for most people to follow and to incorporate into their daily lives. How many times have you seen someone lose a lot of weight in a short period and heard people say, "Have you seen so-and-so, since she's been on that new diet? She looks so good." Then you see that person a year or later, and she is heavier than ever. That's the typical outcome of a fad diet.

The key to eating healthy over the long-term is balance and moderation in the foods you consume daily. You can eat any food you desire as long as it is in moderation and balanced it with the rest of the foods you consume. For example, I love brownies, so when I have a brownie for dessert I only have one. I also balance the carbohydrates and sugar in the brownie by not having bread with my meal.

The first step to learning balance and moderation in your diet is knowing how to classify foods into their basic source of protein, carbohydrates, and fats as well as how they are used in your body. The second step is mastering portion size. Knowing how many calories you consume from each food source and what your serving sizes are will enable you to balance your meals. Eating this way can be easily incorporated into your lifestyle—it's a plan you can stick with over time.

So let's begin by seeing how foods are broken down into their basic components of protein, carbohydrates, and fats and how your body uses them.

Protein

Protein is a necessary part of every living cell in your body. Next to water, protein comprises the greatest portion of your body weight. Protein substances make up your muscles, ligaments, tendons, organs, glands, nails, hair, and many vital body fluids. It is essential for the growth, repair, and healing of your bones, tissues, and cells. In addition, the enzymes and hormones that catalyze and regulate your body processes are comprised of protein. So you see the proper amount of protein in your diet is vital for your health and wellbeing.

Protein is composed of building-block chemicals called amino acids. There are approximately 28 commonly known amino acids that your body uses to create all the various combinations of proteins needed for survival. These 28 commonly known amino acids are further classified as essential and nonessential amino acids. Nonessential amino acids can be produced in your body, while essential amino acids cannot be produced in your body and must be obtained from the foods you eat.

The sources of protein in your diet are classified as complete or incomplete. Complete proteins contain all the essential amino acids and are mostly from animal sources such as meat, fish, poultry, eggs, and dairy products. Incomplete proteins lack one or more essential amino acids that your body cannot make itself. Incomplete proteins usually come from plant-based sources such as fruits, vegetables, grains, and nuts. You must eat incomplete sources of protein in a combination that contains all the essential amino acids in order for your body to use them.

As mentioned, you must get your essential amino acids from your diet because your body cannot make them itself. Some of the best animal sources of protein are fish, poultry, lean cuts of meat, and low-fat dairy products. Some of the best vegetable sources are beans, nuts, and whole grains.

Protein's Effect on Aging

Getting enough protein in your diet is crucial for building and maintaining muscle mass especially as you age. As I mentioned earlier, losing muscle mass is very detrimental to your health. Age-related muscle loss known as sacopenia can begin in your thirties and accelerate with age if left unabated. Sacopenia can lead to muscle weakness, fatigue, insulin resistance, body fat accumulation, injury, and many other problems we associate with aging.

Increased protein consumption, and strength training are two of the most effective ways to combat muscle loss. While 0.8 grams of protein per kilogram of body weight (0.36 grams per pound) has been the normal recommendation for daily protein intake, new studies show that 1 to 1.5 grams of protein per kilogram of body weight (0.45 to 0.68 grams per pound) may be more beneficial in building, maintaining, and reducing muscle loss.

Protein quality, quantity, and timing of consumption throughout the day, in conjunction with physical activity, are all important to the building and maintenance of muscle mass. The goal of protein consumption and lean muscle mass is to optimize muscle protein synthesis (the biological process by which muscle cells are regenerated). Studies now show consuming 25 to 30 grams of high quality protein at each meal (breakfast, lunch, and dinner) is necessary to stimulate maximal protein synthesis.

Protein's Effect on Weight Loss

Scientific research is now revealing that people who consume higher amounts of protein (20 to 30 percent of their daily caloric intake), while cutting back on their carbohydrate intake, tend to lose weight faster and stay leaner than those people on low-fat diets.

The reason higher protein, lower carbohydrates diets are more conducive to weight loss and maintenance is interesting. First, high-protein foods slow the movement of food from the stomach to the intestines, meaning you feel full longer and don't get hungry as often. Second, protein has a leveling effect on your blood sugar which means you are less likely to get spikes in your blood sugar that lead to cravings for carbohydrates. Third, your body uses more energy to digest protein than it does to digest fat or carbohydrates.

Getting the proper amount of protein at breakfast is especially important if you are trying to lose weight. Breakfast is the first meal of the day and what you eat determines whether you start your day in fat burning or fat storage mode.

Eating a breakfast rich in carbohydrates and low in protein (the typical American breakfast) starts your day in fat storage mode. The cereal, bread, fruit, and juice you have for breakfast are all carbohydrate-based and are converted into sugar by your body, thus causing a spike in your blood sugar. Then your body produces insulin to take that blood sugar and store it in your body mostly as body fat. Soon after your blood sugar drops and you feel famished, and you crave more carbohydrate-based foods which starts a cycle of blood sugar spikes and crashes and its insuring sugar cravings.

On the contrary, having a breakfast that contains the proper amount of high quality protein such as eggs, lean meat, and low fat dairy starts your day in a fat burning mode. As mentioned earlier, consuming 25 to 30 grams of protein is necessary for maximal protein synthesis. This building and repair of muscle cells is very energy intensive and it burns body fat mainly as fuel for this process. Thus, having 25 to 30 grams of protein at breakfast activates muscle cell regeneration and also alleviates blood sugar spikes which lead to cravings.

Now that you know how important protein is for you, here are some good sources of protein listed by the U.S. Department of Agriculture to help you get the proper amount in your daily diet.

1 ounce meat, fish, or poultry equals 7 grams of protein
1 large egg equals 6 grams of protein
4 ounces milk equal 4 grams of protein
4 ounces low-fat yogurt equals 6 grams of protein
4 ounces soy milk equals 5 grams of protein
3 ounces tofu, firm equals 13 grams of protein
1 ounce cheese equals 7 grams of protein
1/2 cup low-fat cottage cheese equals 14 grams of protein
1/2 cup cooked kidney beans equals 7 grams of protein
1/2 cup lentils equals 9 grams of protein
1 ounce nuts equals 7 grams of protein
2 tablespoons peanut butter equals 8 grams of protein
1/2 cup vegetables equals 2 grams of protein
1 slice bread equals 2 grams of protein
1/2 cup of most grains/pastas equals 2 grams of protein

Carbohydrates

The popularity of the Atkins, South Beach, and other low-carbohydrate diets has probably led you to believe that carbohydrates are "bad" for you. Just reading the hype in the media would make you think that carbohydrates are the cause of the obesity epidemic in the United States.

It's true: eating a lot of easily-digested carbohydrates from white bread, white rice, pastries, sugared sodas, and other highly processed foods may contribute to your weight gain and, therefore interfere with your efforts to lose weight. On the contrary, consuming whole grains, beans, fruits, vegetables, and other intact carbohydrates promotes good health. As I mentioned before, a healthy diet is about balance and moderation. A basic knowledge of what carbohydrates are and how your body uses them is essential to understanding how to balance them in your diet.

Carbohydrates are essential nutrients that are excellent sources of energy (measured as calories) for your body; they are the preferred fuel for your brain and nervous system. Carbohydrates are found in an array of foods such as bread, beans, milk, popcorn, potatoes, cookies, spaghetti, soft drinks, corn, and desserts. The most common and abundant forms are classified as sugars, fibers, and starches.

The basic building block of every carbohydrate is a sugar molecule, a simple union of carbon, hydrogen, and oxygen. Starches and fibers forms of carbohydrates are essentially chains of sugar molecules.

As mentioned above, most carbohydrates come from plant sources and are in the form of sugars, starches, and fibers. Sugars, also called simple carbohydrates, include fruit sugar (fructose), corn or grape sugar (dextrose or glucose), and table sugar (sucrose). Starches, also known as complex carbohydrates, include everything made of three or more linked sugars. Starches include foods such as breads, cereals, grains, pasta, rice, and flour. Fibers are technically classified as a starch because they are complex carbohydrates that your body cannot break down into sugar molecules. Fibers are more abundant in whole grains, legumes, and vegetables.

Your body breaks down all carbohydrates, except for fibers, into single sugar molecules regardless of their source. These simple sugars are further converted into glucose, also known as blood sugar. Your body is designed to use blood sugar as a universal source of fuel for energy.

Fiber is the form of carbohydrate that your body cannot break down into simple sugar molecules. It passes through your body undigested. Fiber comes in two varieties: soluble, which dissolves in water, and insoluble, which does not. Although neither type provides energy for your body, they both promote health in many ways. Soluble fiber binds to fatty substances in your intestines and carries them out as waste, thus lowering your low-density lipoprotein (LDL, or bad cholesterol). It also helps regulate your body's use of sugars, helping you to keep your hunger and blood sugar in check. Insoluble fiber helps push food through your intestinal tract, promoting regularity and helping to prevent constipation.

Here's what happens when you eat a food containing carbohydrates. Your digestive system breaks down the digestible ones into sugar, which then enters your blood. As your blood sugar level rises, special cells in your pancreas churn out insulin, a hormone that signals your cells to absorb the blood sugar for energy or for storage. As your cells soak up the blood sugar, its level in your bloodstream begins to fall. Now, your pancreas starts making another hormone called glucagon, which signals your liver to start releasing stored blood sugar. This interplay of insulin and glucagon ensures that cells throughout your body have a steady supply of blood sugar.

Maintaining a steady blood sugar level is a very important component of your diet. While you've just seen that your body breaks down all digestible carbohydrates into blood sugar, some are converted into blood sugar faster than others. Thus, some carbohydrates cause a spike in your blood sugar level causing you to feel hungry faster and to crave more sugary foods. Other carbohydrates are converted into blood sugar more slowly, leveling out your blood sugar and resulting in less hunger and food cravings.

For this reason, the Glycemic Index (GI) was developed to classify how quickly your body converts carbohydrates into blood sugar as opposed to pure glucose. Glucose has a GI of 100, and all other carbohydrate-based foods are ranked against it. Foods with a score of 70 or more are considered to have a high GI, while those with a score of 55 or less are considered low.

Eating lots of food with a high GI causes spikes in your blood sugar level, this can lead to many health issues, such as type 2 diabetes, heart disease, and obesity. Eating low GI foods causes your blood sugar level to stay steady thus keeping your energy level balanced and causing you to feel fuller longer between meals. The following are some additional benefits of eating low GI carbohydrates.

- Helps you to lose and manage your weight
- Increases your body's sensitivity to insulin
- Decreases your risk of developing type 2 diabetes
- Reduces your risk of heart disease
- Improves your blood cholesterol levels
- Reduces hunger and keeps you fuller longer
- Helps you prolong physical activity
- Helps you to refuel your carbohydrate stores after exercise

You can get the GI rating of hundreds of carbohydrate-based foods from the Glycemic Index Foundation, sponsored by the University of Sydney in Australia. It maintains a searchable database of more than 1600 entries at http://www.glycemicindex.com.

The GI is interesting because some of the foods you think would have a high rating actually do not. For instance, fructose, or fruit sugar has a minimal effect on blood sugar, while white bread and French-fried potatoes are converted to blood sugar nearly as fast as pure glucose. In other words, you can't classify foods as having a high or low GI based on the sweetness of taste. Many factors affect a food's GI such as:

- Processing: Grains that have been milled and refined have a higher GI
- Type of starch: Starches come in many different configurations. Some are easier to break into sugar molecules than others. For example, starch in potatoes is digested and absorbed into the bloodstream relatively quickly.
- Fiber content: The sugars in fiber are linked in a way that is hard for your body to break down. Thus, the more fiber a food has the less digestible carbohydrate, and consequently, the less sugar it can deliver into your blood stream.
- Fat and acid content: The more fat or acid a food contains, the slower its carbohydrates are converted to sugar and absorbed into your bloodstream.
- Physical form: Finely ground grain is more rapidly digested, and so it has a higher GI than more coarsely ground grain.

The basic technique for eating the low GI way is simply a "this-for-that" approach. In other words, swap high GI carbohydrates for low GI carbohydrates. You don't need to count numbers or do any mental arithmetic to make sure you are eating a healthy, low GI diet. Follow these easy to implement suggestions.

- Use breakfast cereals based on oats, barley and bran
- Use breads with whole-grains, stone-ground flour, or sourdough
- Reduce the amount of potatoes you eat
- Enjoy all types of fruit and vegetables
- Use brown rice
- Enjoy whole-wheat pasta and noodles
- Eat plenty of salad vegetables with a vinaigrette dressing

As you see, it's important to include the right kind of carbohydrates as part of your daily intake. Now you ask, how many grams of carbohydrates can I eat daily? This depends on factors such as your age, gender, body composition, physical activity level, and metabolic health. Thus, there are no one-size-fits all answers.

People who are physically active, and have more muscle mass need more carbohydrates than people who are sedentary and have less muscle mass. People who have metabolic issues such as obesity and type 2 diabetes cannot tolerate the same amount of carbohydrates as people who are in good health.

Here are some general guidelines for daily carbohydrate intake if weight loss is your goal. For moderate weight loss (around 2 lbs per week), eat 50-100 grams of low to medium glycemic carbohydrates per day. For gradual weight loss and maintenance (1-1.5 lbs per week) consume 100-150 grams of low to medium glycemic carbohydrates daily.

Because I have a lot of muscle mass and I'm also very active I generally consume about 210 grams of low to medium glycemic carbohydrates daily. I find that this amount gives me plenty of energy for all my daily activities. You'll find that eating low to medium GI carbohydrates levels out your energy and keeps you from those high and low points throughout the day.

Fat

Fat has also taken a bad rap over the years, but it is very essential to your health and well-being. Again, balance and moderation is the key.

For decades, the mantra for healthy eating has been "eat a low-fat, low-cholesterol diet." Touted as a way to lose weight and prevent heart disease and other chronic conditions, millions of people have followed this advice. Seeing a tremendous marketing opportunity, food companies re-engineered thousands of foods to be low-fat or fat-free. The low-fat approach to eating may have made a difference for the occasional individual, but as a nation, it has neither helped us control our weight nor has it helped us become healthier. In the 1960s, fats and oils supplied Americans with about 45 percent of their calories. About 13 percent of the population was obese and less than one percent had type 2 diabetes. Today, Americans take in less fat, getting about 33 percent of calories from fats and oils; yet 34 percent of the population is obese, and eight percent has diabetes (mostly type 2).[3]

Research has shown that the total amount of fat in your diet is not linked to

[3] Harvard School of Public Health

weight or disease. What actually matters is the type of fat in your diet. Trans fats and saturated fats increase your risk of cardiovascular disease, while monounsaturated and polyunsaturated fats do just the opposite. But then you ask, "What about cholesterol in food?" The answer is, for most people the mix of fats in their diets influences cholesterol in their bloodstreams far more than cholesterol in food.

Almost all foods contain some fat. Even foods like carrots and lettuce contain small amounts of fat. That's a testament to how important fats are for your health and well-being. Fat provides a terrific source of energy for your body as well as a great depot for storing it. It is an important part of cell membranes, helping govern what gets into and out of your cells. Your body uses cholesterol as the starting point to make estrogen, testosterone, vitamin D, and other vital compounds. Fats are also biologically active molecules that can influence how your muscles respond to insulin. Also, different types of fats can fire-up or cool down inflammation in your body.

Your body packages fat and cholesterol into tiny protein-covered particles called lipoproteins in order to get them into your blood stream. Some of these lipoproteins are big and fluffy, while others are small and dense. However, the most important ones to remember for your health and well-being are low-density lipoproteins, high-density lipoproteins, and triglycerides as explained below.

Low-density lipoproteins (LDL) carry cholesterol from your liver to the rest of your body. Your cells latch onto these particles and extract fat and cholesterol from them. When there is too much LDL cholesterol in your blood, these particles can form deposits in the walls of your coronary arteries and other arteries throughout your body. These deposits, called plaque can cause your arteries to narrow and limit blood flow, resulting in a heart attack or stroke. Thus, LDL cholesterol is called your bad cholesterol.

High-density lipoproteins (HDL) scavenge cholesterol from your bloodstream, your LDL, and your artery walls and ferry it back to your liver for disposal. Thus, HDL cholesterol is referred to as your good cholesterol.

Triglycerides comprise most of the fat that you eat and that travels through your bloodstream. Because triglycerides are your body's main vehicle for transporting fats to your cells, they are essential for good health. However, an excess of triglycerides can be unhealthy.

The type of fat in your diet determines to a large extent the amount of total and LDL cholesterol in your bloodstream. Cholesterol in food matters too, but not nearly as much. You can basically break the fats in your diet into three categories; good, bad, and very bad.

Good Fats

Unsaturated fats are called good fats because they can improve blood cholesterol levels, ease inflammation, stabilize heart rhythms, and play a number of other beneficial roles. Unsaturated fats are predominantly found in foods derived from plants, such as vegetable oils, nuts, and seeds. They are liquid at room temperature.

Furthermore, there are two types of unsaturated fats: monounsaturated and polyunsaturated. Monounsaturated fats are found in high concentrations in canola, peanut, and olive oil, in avocados, nuts like almonds, hazelnuts, and pecans, and seeds such as pumpkin and sesame. Polyunsaturated fats are found in high concentrations in sunflower, corn, soybean and flaxseed oil. They also are found in foods such as walnuts, flaxseeds and fish.

Research has shown that replacing carbohydrates in your diet with good fats reduces harmful levels of LDL and increases protective HDL in your bloodstream. A randomized trial called the Optimal Macronutrient Intake Trial for Heart Health showed that replacing a carbohydrate-rich diet with one rich in unsaturated fat—predominantly monounsaturated fats—lowers blood pressure, improves lipid levels, and reduces the estimated cardiovascular risk.

Bad Fats

Saturated fats are called bad fats because they increase your total cholesterol level by elevating harmful LDL. Your body can produce all the saturated fat that it needs, so you don't have to get any from your diet. In the U.S. and other developed countries, saturated fats come mainly from meat, seafood, poultry with skin, and whole-milk dairy products. A few plant sources, such as coconuts and coconut oil, palm oil and palm kernel oil, also are high in saturated fats.

As a general rule, it's good to keep your intake of saturated fats as low as possible. Saturated fats are found in many foods, including vegetable oils (that are mainly unsaturated fats), so you cannot completely eliminate them from your diet. Because red meat and dairy fat are the main sources of saturated fats for most people, minimizing them in your diet is the primary way to reduce your intake of saturated fat.

Very Bad Fats

Trans fatty acids, more commonly known as trans fats, are made by heating liquid vegetable oils in the presence of hydrogen gas—a process called hydrogenation. Partially hydrogenating vegetable oils makes them more stable and less likely to spoil. It also converts the oil into a solid which makes transportation easier. Partially hydrogenated oils can also withstand repeated heating without breaking down, making them ideal for frying fast foods. This is the reason partially hydrogenated oils have been a mainstay in restaurants and the food industry.

Trans fats are worse for cholesterol levels than saturated fats because they raise bad LDL and lower good HDL. They also increase inflammation, an over-activity of the immune system that is associated with heart disease, stroke, diabetes, and other chronic conditions. Even small amounts of trans fats in your diet can have harmful health effects. For every extra two percent of daily calories from trans fat (the amount in a medium order of fast food French fries) the risk of coronary heart disease increases by 23 percent. It is estimated that eliminating trans fats from the U.S. food supply would prevent between six and 19 percent of heart attacks and heart attack-related deaths (more than 200,000) each year.

Recommendations for Fat in Your Diet

Are you confused at this point about the type of fats and their varied effects on your health? If so, remember to replace the bad fats in your diet with the good fats. Here are some suggestions to help you limit the bad fats in your diet.

- Eliminate trans fats from partially hydrogenated oils. Check food labels for the presence of trans fats and avoid fried fast foods.
- Limit your intake of saturated fats by cutting back on red meat and full-fat dairy products. When possible replace red meat with poultry, fish, beans, and nuts. Also, try switching from whole milk and other full-fat dairy foods to lower-fat versions.
- Use liquid vegetable oils rich in polyunsaturated and monounsaturated fats in place of butter in your cooking and at the table.
- Eat one or more sources of omega-3 fats every day. Good sources are fish, walnuts, canola or soybean oil, ground flax seeds and flaxseed oil.

Water

Water constitutes the largest part of your body. Most people don't drink enough water daily. If you are even mildly dehydrated, your metabolism may slow down. In one study, adults who drank eight or more glasses of water a day burned more calories than those who drank four. To stay hydrated, drink a glass of water or other unsweetened beverage before every meal and snack. In addition, try munching on fresh fruits and vegetables, which are full of fluid, rather than pretzels or chips. I suggest you drink at least 64 ounces of water daily.

My Typical Diet

Here's an example of how I balance my diet. Each day, I typically consume around 2300 calories consisting of approximately 210 grams of low to medium glycemic carbohydrates, 160 grams of high quality protein, and 80 grams of fat mostly from walnuts (high in omega-3 fat). Here's my typical day:

Breakfast: I usually have 16 ounces of water as soon as I wake up. Then, I have a protein shake (whey protein) made of frozen blueberries, ice and almond milk. I also have one cup of oatmeal.

Mid morning snack: Around 9:00, I usually have about 2 ounces of raw walnuts, and a medium sized apple.

Lunch: I typically have about six ounces of chicken, fish, or lean meat, a medium size baked sweet potato, and steamed vegetables.

Mid afternoon snack: Around 3:00, I usually have about 2 ounces of raw walnuts, and a medium sized apple.

Dinner: I typically have about 6 ounces of chicken, fish, or lean meat, a serving of a low to medium GI carbohydrate, and a garden salad.

In addition, I drink at least 64 ounce of water every day. I can't overestimate the importance of hydration in your diet. Your body needs water to process calories. As previously mentioned, if you are even mildly dehydrated, your metabolism may slow down.

As you can see, I eat about every three hours. When you eat large meals with many hours between them, you train your metabolism to slow down. Having a small meal or snack every three to four hours keeps your metabolism cranking, so you burn more calories throughout the day. Several studies have also shown that people who snack regularly eat less at meal time.

I follow this diet Monday through Friday. On Saturday and Sunday I enjoy a cheeseburger, desserts, or any other food that I have a taste for. It's easy for me to stick to my diet during the week when I know that I can loosen up a bit on the weekend. This way of eating has worked well for me for more than 20 years.

In Summary

Life is meant to be enjoyed. Part of the joy of living is enjoying good food. On the other hand, if you don't have good health, how can you enjoy life? The task is creating a healthy lifestyle in which you don't deprive yourself of the things that you love and enjoy. This is what balance and moderation is all about. With knowledge comes power, and I hope I have given you enough basic information about food for you to choose a healthy diet that you can live with for the rest of your life.

9 CONCLUSION

There is a way of living that I call the top down approach in which things flow easily and harmoniously in your life. It starts with recognizing that you are more than just a physical body. There is more to you that is unseen than there is visible. You are the energy of invisible spirit and mind made visible into flesh.

When you let the energy of your spirit govern, guard, and guide your life everything takes its proper place and you find happiness and fulfillment in all that you do. Isn't that all that you want anyway?

"Seek ye first the kingdom of God and His righteousness and all these things shall be added unto you." —Matthew 6:33.

ABOUT THE AUTHORS

Darvis R. Simms grew up the son of a sharecropper on a small farm in eastern North Carolina. As a result of his upbringing he learned the value of education and determination as a way to change his life conditions. After earning a degree in mechanical engineering, Darvis went on to work in the corporate world for over 16 years before deciding to pursue his passion of helping others through personal training, which he has been successfully doing for over 20 years.

Through his journey in personal training Darvis witnessed how his clients' beliefs in the negative aspects of aging affected the outcome of their fitness results. This prompted Darvis to write *Forever Fit and Firm*, a book showing that healthy lifestyle habits and a positive mental outlook lead to healthy aging.

Darvis says, "In the writing of *Balanced Life* it is my hope to awaken people to their inner beauty and power."

Alisha Lalji had an abnormal life compared to most North American families. On top of her unusual circumstances, Alisha dealt with the everyday hardships most of us face. In a quest to answer life's tougher questions, the universe took Alisha on a transformative journey of the skin, body, mind, spirit, and soul through exploration of the healing arts. This journey was one of introspection, liberation, truth, freedom, illumination, and above all true happiness.

Holistically healing clients using ancient practices, a scientific understanding, and the power of Alchemy Theta Therapies (pioneered by Alisha and Tom Partridge), Alisha hopes to awaken and empower all to realize their unlimited potential. Above all else, Alisha is passionate about spreading knowledge on how our thoughts and intentions can bring about great abundance and love, all while having the power to transform the world.

Please contact Darvis for more information and speaking engagements at darvis@foreverfitfirm.com.

To learn more about Alisha's healing modalities, please visit www.EMLuxurySpa.com.